EVERYDAY WISDOM

D R.   W A Y N E   W.   D Y E R

HAY HOUSE, INC.
Carson, CA

EVERYDAY WISDOM
by Dr. Wayne W. Dyer

Copyright © 1993 by Dr. Wayne W. Dyer

Library of Congress Cataloging-in-Publication Data

Dyer, Wayne W.
    Everyday wisdom / Wayne W. Dyer.
       p.   cm.
    ISBN 1-56170-076-2 (pbk.) : $5.95
    1. Conduct of life—Quotations, maxims, etc. I. Title.
BJ1581.2.D884 1993   93–36208
170'.44—dc20   CIP

Library of Congress Catalog Card No. 93–36208
ISBN: 1-56170-076-2

Internal design by David Butler
Typesetting by Freedmen's Organization, Los Angeles, CA 90004

93 94 95 96 97 98   10 9 8 7 6 5 4 3 2 1
First Printing, October 1993

Published and Distributed in the United States by:
Hay House, Inc.
P.O. Box 6204
Carson, CA 90749-6204

Printed in the United States of America
on Recycled Paper

To Barbara Bergen
With Appreciation and Love

You are not a human being
having a spiritual
experience.
You are a spiritual being
having a human experience.

All the abundance you want is already here. You just have to tune it in.

Three things clog your soul—negativity—judgement—and imbalance.

Everything in the universe flows. You can't get ahold of water by clutching it. Let your hand relax, and you can experience it.

The whole universal system is held together through love, harmony and cooperation. If you use your thoughts according to these principles you can transcend anything that gets in the way.

Perhaps you'll be surprised to learn that there is no such thing as a nervous breakdown. Nerves don't break down. People choose to.

Having a plan is not necessarily unhealthy, but falling in love with the plan is a real neurosis . . . don't let your plan become bigger than you.

Thoughts, when properly nourished and internalized, will become a reality in your world of form. Thoughts are extremely powerful things.

Ultimately, there is nothing to forgive, because there is nothing to judge and no one to blame.

Positive thoughts keep you in harmony with the universe.

Traffic, in itself, can never irritate anybody. It just does what it does. Traffic doesn't care!

We can only give away
to others what we have
inside ourselves.

Be willing to let anything happen.

Each time you send love in response to hate,
you diffuse the hate.

Forgiveness is an act of self-love.

If you step back far enough, it is easy to see humanity as one.

What you see is evidence of what you believe. Believe it and you'll see it.

All of your behavior results from the thoughts that precede it.

In reality it is much easier *not* to smoke or eat chocolate than to do so. It is your mind that convinces you otherwise.

Anything you must have comes to own you. Ironically, when you release it, you start getting more of it.

In order to make a visualization a reality in the world of form, you must be *willing* to do whatever it takes to make it happen.

Whatever the question, love is the answer.

I once gave the refrigerator repairman several of my books and tapes. The repairman asked, "How do you ever expect to make any money when you give away all your stuff?" I replied, "When the day comes that you don't have to ask me that question, you'll have the answer."

Nothing is formed.
Nothing dies.
Everything is simply
in transition.

If you control your thoughts, and your feelings come from your thoughts, then you control your feelings.

If you only believe what you see, then you are limited to what's on the surface. If you only believe what you see, why do you pay your electric bill?

If you are to change a habit, you must *be* the treatment.

No one can create anger or stress within you. Only you can do that by virtue of how you process your world.

"No limit people" don't say, "I'm going to get it all." They say, "I am it all already, but I can grow."

No one knows enough to be a pessimist.

No amount of guilt can ever change history. No amount of guilt can ever change anything.

Blame is a neat little device that you can use whenever you don't want to take responsibility for something in your life. Use it and you will avoid all risks and impede your own growth.

Make a personal commitment to do what you love and love what you do. Today!

BE the cure. Don't look outside yourself for it.

If prayer is you talking to
God, then intuition is
God talking to you.

Listen to those inner signals that help you make the right choices—no matter what anyone thinks.

Trust your intuitive voices and go with them.

Learn to find the blessing in pain. Practice observing the pain rather than owning it.

Loving sacredly means loving what is, even if you don't comprehend the deeper meaning behind it.

Behavior is a much better barometer of what you are than words.

I am grateful to all those people who said "No." It is because of them that I did it all myself.

Every obstacle is an opportunity. Every obstacle is a test.

Emotions are choices.

Doing what you love is the cornerstone of having abundance in your life.

Deficiency-motivated people spend their lives in the disease called *more*—always trying to acquire something to make themselves feel complete and to repair the deficiency.

Conflict is a violation of harmony. If you participate in it you are part of the problem, not the solution.

Don't let emotions
immobilize you.
View them as choices.

Each place along the way is somewhere you had to be to be here.

Don't be impatient with the universe.

In God's eyes no one on this planet is any better than you.

Realize that the journey and the goal are always the same.

Detachment is the absence of a need to hold on to anyone or anything. It is a way of thinking and being which gives us the freedom to flow with life. Detachment is the only vehicle available to take you from striving to arriving.

Do what you want, as long as you're not interfering with anyone else's right to do the same —this is the definition of morality.

So many people are *expecting* a miracle instead of *being* a miracle.

Being bored is a choice. There is no such thing as boredom in the world.

Death is nothing to fear. It is only another dimension.

If one of us succeeds, we all do.

I send my tennis opponent love. It removes the negative from my game.

You will be trapped
emotionally and physically
until you learn to forgive.

I will fill myself with love, and I will send that out into the world. How others treat me is their path, how I react is mine.

It is a simple procedure to calculate the number of seeds in an apple. But who among us can ever say how many apples are in a seed?

Injustice is a constant, but you can refuse to be seduced into being emotionally immobilized over it.

In the world of pure thought there are no boundaries, hence no limits.

I recommend being gentle with yourself and loving yourself unconditionally, regardless of what comes your way.

I finally realized that other people are simply going to be exactly the way they are, independent of my opinion about them.

How could you ever have owned anything at all? The best that we can do is to have temporary possession of our toys for a tiny speck of time.

I have a suit in my closet with the pocket cut out. It is a reminder to me that I won't be taking anything with me. The last suit I wear won't need any pockets.

You are the sum total of all your choices up until this moment.

Everything in the universe is connected through thought.

Enlightenment is your ego's greatest disappointment.

You cannot always control
what goes on outside,
but you can always control
what goes on inside.

Give for the sake of giving and keep it circulating as it flows back.

Fill yourself with love for everyone. See the unfolding of God in everyone you meet including those whom you have been taught to reject.

Fighting weakens while harmony strengthens and empowers.

Harmony gets inside you through your thinking. The ancestor to all action is a thought.

Everything you are against can be restated in a way that puts you in support of something. Instead of being against war, be for peace. Instead of being against poverty, be for prosperity. Instead of joining a war on drugs, be for purity in our youth.

Every man-made action starts with a thought, an idea, a vision, a mental image. From there it materializes into form.

If the world were so organized that everything had to be fair, no living creature could survive for a day. The birds would be forbidden to eat worms, and everyone's self-interest would have to be served.

It is love and cooperation that makes it all work.

In the world of form, blame is a convenient excuse for why our world is not exactly what we would like it to be. The state of the world is a reflection of our state of mind.

In the East they contemplate the forest. In the West they count the trees.

In the context of eternity,
time does not matter.

There is nothing to worry about—ever! Either you have control or you don't. If you do, then take control. If you don't, then dismiss it. Don't waste your energy on worry.

There is no way to happiness. Happiness is the way. There is no way to prosperity. Prosperity is the way.

It's more important for you to *BE* than to have a goal.

Be in this moment. There has always only been *NOW*.

The process of surrendering, focusing and living on purpose leads to ecstasy.

It's easy to love some people. The true test is to love someone who's hard to love. Send all your enemies love.

When a problem arises, go within. Get very quiet about it. Use it to learn something.

Being intelligent is not being studious. It is knowing how to be fulfilled in all circumstances.

Yesterday is just as over as the Peloponnesian war.

You are creating it all. Nobody else is doing it to you.

Go beyond the ideas of succeeding and failing —these are the judgements. Stay in the process and allow the universe to handle the details.

When you squeeze an orange you get orange juice because that's what's inside. The very same principle is true about you. When someone squeezes you—puts pressure on you—what comes out is what's inside. And if you don't like what's inside you can change it by changing your thoughts.

Stop focusing on what you do not have and shift your consciousness to an appreciation for all you are and all that you do have.

Some people think they are their packaging. Your body is nothing more than your garage where you temporarily park your soul.

Stop looking for your purpose. *BE* it!

Tell me what you are for, and I will show you what is going to expand in a positive way. Tell me what you are against, and I will show you what is going to expand in a destructive way.

The essence of greatness is the ability to choose personal fulfillment in circumstances where others choose madness.

The fear of not *HAVING* enough prevents many from seeing that they already *ARE* enough.

You are totally free when you are able to stop thinking about yourself and your self-importance.

The more you give away, the more you get back.

The only boundaries we have are in form. There are no obstacles in thought.

The only response to hatred is love. Everything else will bring you down.

You can sit forever, lamenting
about how bad you've been,
feeling guilty until your death,
and not one tiny slice of that
guilt will do anything to
rectify past behavior.

You are the result of all the previous pictures you have painted for yourself . . . and you can always paint new ones.

All you get is today, and next week maybe. But today, for sure.

You can't get ahold of the wind. It's the same with thought.

You can't age thought. You can only age form.

Attachment to being right creates suffering. When you have a choice to be right or to be kind, choose "kind" and watch your suffering disappear.

Anything that immobilizes you, gets in your way, keeps you from your goals, is all yours. You can throw it away anytime you choose.

What you must do to move yourself into the mental framework for "miracle making" is to just let go.

Once you believe in yourself, and see your soul as divine and precious, you will automatically be converted to a being who can create a miracle.

Authentic empowerment is the knowing that you are on purpose, doing God's work, peacefully and harmoniously.

Are you part of the problem or part of the solution?

One cannot choose up sides on a round planet.

Authentic empowerment is surrendering to that which is loving, harmonious and good in ourselves, and not allowing for enemies in our consciousness.

Jesus told you that even the least among us could do all that he had done, and ever greater things. You can be a miracle worker.

If you doubt the principles of the universe, they will not work for you.

To not forgive is to not understand how the universe works and how you fit into it.

Giving is in alignment with your purpose.

You cannot own anything while you are here.
You cannot acquire anything. Your life can
only be given away.

Love empowers you to higher levels.

What you think about expands. If your thoughts are centered on "What's missing?", then "What's missing?", by definition, will have to expand.

Nothing you imagine in your mind is impossible.

What goes around, comes around.

Even in a prison, your corner of freedom is how you choose to think. No one can take that away ever!

Meditation shatters the illusion of your separateness.

Meditation gives you an opportunity to come to know your invisible self.

Your lifetime in form is to be
honored and celebrated.
Go beyond your enslavement
and live fully in the now
as this is the only time
you have.

Once you have learned how to enter your inner kingdom, you have a special retreat within that is always available to you.

Everything exists for some reason as a part of the perfect intelligence that is the universe.

More is less, less is more.

You are here for a reason, and it is *not* to hoard a lot of physical stuff.

Rather than put a label on yourself as Christian, Jew, Moslem, Buddhist, or whatever, instead make a commitment to be Christ-like, God-like, Buddha-like and Mohammed-like.

There is no stress in the world, only people thinking stressful thoughts.

No one can create anger or stress within you, only you can do that by virtue of how you process your world.

How can one invisible thought be more or less valuable than another invisible thought?

Your inner and outer design is perfectly in balance with all things in the universe.

The universe provides abundantly when you are in a state of gratefulness.

When you *KNOW* rather than *BELIEVE*, you will discover the necessary abilities to carry out your purpose. Beliefs are handed to you, hence they are received with some doubt. Knowing comes from within.

When you know and feel the miracle that you are, you become certain that nothing is impossible for you.

There is magic in knowing that transcends logic.

You can never fail. You just produce results.

Willingness to forgive yourself is the necessary step to being in harmony with all of the universal principles.

Prosperity is about process. Process is about purpose. Purpose is about loving and giving.

In regard to addictions, when you are pursuing poisons, you can never get enough of what you don't want. You become what you think about all day long and those days eventually become your lifetime.

If you meet someone whose soul is not aligned with yours, send them love and move along.

If you are going to follow your bliss and make a difference in the world, you will soon learn that you cannot follow the herd.

All of the great teachers have left us with a similar message: Go within, discover your invisible higher self, and know God as the love that is within you.

It is in every one of us to be love, if we allow it.

A new attitude can convert
a stifling job situation
to one of joy.

One song! That is our uni (one) verse (song). No matter how we separate into individual notes, we are all still involved in the one song.

One small voice within the "universal onesong" can influence the entire being toward destruction or harmony.

Everything is synchronized and working perfectly in the universal onesong.

When you judge others, you do not define them, you define yourself.

Our suffering is caused by the mind—by a mind that insists on having preferences and will not allow others to be just as they are.

True joy and the exhilarating feeling of being at peace with yourself and your world comes to the person who lets his or her physical world flow from the pleadings of the soul.

Shift from form to spirit. Know the will of the Father and fall back in the knowing.

Align yourself to your soul, listen to those inner pleadings to be at ease and on purpose. It is in this mind-set that real magic will become available to you.

You are not stuck where you are unless you decide to be.

If you wonder about the difference between attachment and enjoyment, ask yourself how you would react if suddenly an object you valued was gone.

Those who think that
the world is a dark place
are blind to the light
that might illuminate
their lives.

For every act of unkindness there are a million kind acts.

Always remember that each day as you look at your world and see millions upon millions of flowers opening up, God does it all without using any force.

If an event happens, it cannot unhappen in your physical world.

You can't get prune juice from an orange, no matter how hard you squeeze it. You can't give hate if you only have love inside.

You will be happy to know that the universal law that created miracles has not been repealed.

When you call "yourself" a jerk, that is your invisible "critic" judging your outer self. Remember, what you think about, expands.

You come into this world in a naked little body, and you leave in a large wrinkled body . . . if you're lucky.

There is one grand lie—that we are limited. The only limits we have are the limits we believe.

Since your mind is your own private territory you can give any new idea a private audition for a few days before sharing it with others.

A mind at peace, a mind focused on not harming others, is stronger than any physical force in the universe.

Prosperity is
located within.

Of all the deathbed regrets that I have heard not one of them has been, "I wish I had spent more time at the office."

Be patient and loving with every fearful thought. Practice observing your fears as a witness and you'll see them dissolve.

When you trust in yourself, you trust in the wisdom that created you.

Our lives are what our thoughts create.

All of your doubts are obstacles inhibiting your entry into the kingdom of real magic.

Let go of the notion that things shouldn't be that way. They *ARE* that way!

Nothing is owned, and the sooner you realize this the more you will be able to tune in to the wondrous principle of abundance.

Entering the magic garden of miracles means the emphasis is on developing a consciousness of possibility.

Rulers can remove our outer places of worship, but the inner place, that invisible corner of freedom this is ever present in each of us, can never be legislated.

If you still need a cause and effect explanation, then you will be unable to enter the world of real magic.

Rather than being against evil, be only for love.

The choice is up to you.
It can either be,
"Good morning, God!" or
"Good God, morning."

❖

Our beliefs are the invisible ingredients in all of our activities.

Risks are nothing more than thoughts which you have convinced yourself are impossible to implement.

In order to forgive, you must have blamed.

When you see yourself as connected rather than separate, you automatically begin to cooperate. This is what the healing process is all about.

When you begin to heal the inner you, you alter your immune system.

You create your thoughts, your thoughts create your intentions, and your intentions create your reality.

To know the secret of prosperity, know that you can never find it outside of yourself.

You are never going to get "it" all, you are "it" all already.

You see what you believe, rather than believe what you see.

If it works any place, it works every place.

Give up the "want." Know in your heart that you do not need one more thing to make yourself complete, and then watch all those external things become less and less significant in your heart.

Intuition is
loving guidance.

Your soul, that inner quiet empty space, is yours to consult. It will always guide you in your right direction.

When you know that you are in charge of your intentions, then you will come to know that you are in charge of your entire world.

We put labels on people and fight wars over them. If we truly want harmony, we have to get past the labels.

The *NOW* is the working unit of your life.

Your power and authenticity as a person will not be measured in duration, but in your donations of love.

Death is a very embarrassing event to the ego.

If you find yourself believing that you must always be the way you've always been, you are arguing against growth.

Money—like health, love, happiness and all forms of miraculous happenings that you want to create for yourself—is the result of your living purposefully. It is not a goal unto itself.

You are at once a beating heart and a single heartbeat in this body called humanity.

We are our form and our formlessness. We are both visible and invisible, and we need to honor our totality, not just what we can see and touch.

When you allow God to speak
through you and smile upon
the earth through you—
because you are an unconditional
giver, a purposeful being—
prosperity will be your reward.

Being on purpose means that you are at peace with yourself, and that is what you have to give away.

Neither your family nor your culture gave you your personality. You created it yourself.

Surrender to a new consciousness, a thought that whispers, "I can do this thing in this moment. I will receive all the help that I need as long as I stay with this intention and go within for assistance."

You are eternal, and the invisible essence of you can never die. You have the ability to turn any thought into form with the power of your mind.

You become what you think about.

Your thoughts are all seeds that you plant.

"The kingdom of heaven is within you" is not an empty cliché, it is a reality.

You are already complete and whole, and nothing external to yourself in the physical world can make you more complete.

To be attached to your physical appearance is to ensure a lifetime of suffering as you watch your form go through the natural motions that began the moment of your conception.

Refuse to let an old person move into your body.

Aging is simply a learned way of being.

From the Prince of Peace: "As ye think, so shall ye be."

Real-magic thinkers say,
"I believe it, I know it, and
I will access my spiritual
powers to do it.
It is my intention."

The more you attach your value and humanity to those things outside of yourself, the more you give those things the power to control you.

You are not a human doing but rather a human being.

By concentrating on your breathing, by meditation, and by affirming aloud your intentions, you can reenergize yourself on your life's journey.

Everything you know about yourself corresponds to a belief you are holding.

Would you consult an imaginary fear-based history to make your real-life decisions?

If you are still following a career path that you decided upon as a young person, ask yourself this question today: Would I seek out the advice of a teenager for vocational guidance?

Inner commitment to your own excellence is the stuff of which miracles are made.

Conflict cannot survive without your participation.

Death is a concept that refers to endings. Endings need boundaries, and your dimensionless self has no boundaries.

Empowerment is the inner joy of knowing that external force is not necessary to be at harmony with oneself.

Those who injured us did only
what they knew how to do, given
the conditions of their lives.
If you won't forgive, then
you allow those ancient injuries
to continue their hold on you.

What you think and talk about expands into action.

Look at every obstacle as an opportunity.

Enlightenment demands that you take responsibility for your way of life.

Forgiveness is an act of the heart.

Be consistently aware of the need to serve God and to serve others in any and all of your actions. That is the way of the miracle worker.

Giving and receiving are the same.

God will work with you, not for you.

Everything we fight only weakens us and hinders our ability to see the opportunity in the obstacle.

The entire universe is an intelligence system.

When you are told that you have some kind of physical affliction, you can either prepare to suffer or prepare to heal.

Your will is the gardener
that tends the garden
called your body.
Listen to your body and
it will tell you what
you need to know.

The principles of abundance, synchronicity, detachment and oneness are operative in the universe. All you have to do is tune in to them and let them work through you.

A tree allows the life force to work naturally through it. You have the power within your thoughts to be as natural as the tree.

Spiritual beings keep their thoughts on love and harmony.

Live one day at a time emphasizing ethics rather than rules.

Surrender, trust, and turn away from outer accumulation and achievement and allow yourself to be purposeful and guided.

You, a person with a vision, are like a pebble in a stream, moving ever outward to infinity, impacting on all who come into contact with the ripple.

Intuitive feelings always guide you in a direction of growth and purposefulness.

Within you is the kingdom of serenity that can create all of the prosperity that you could ever want.

Intentions are the energy of your soul coming into contact with your physical reality.

Releasing judgment of another is actually releasing judgment of yourself.

If you can conceive it
in your mind, then it can
be brought into your
physical world.

We send our kids off to school to major in "labeling" and think the ones who do it best deserve the highest grades.

Labels enable you to avoid the hard work and risk of change.

Miracles come in moments. Be ready and willing.

A heart starts beating in a mother's womb six weeks after conception and life as we observe it is under way. It remains a mystery to all of the greatest minds on the planet.

The real measure of your humanity is in your soul.

Anything you desire to do, you can do. Anything!

Your mind is unbound, formless, and infinitely capable of choosing any kind of miracle that it chooses, when it is fully honored and celebrated.

Just as each flower has its own unique color—even though it originates from only *one* light—each individual, although unique in appearance, comes from *one* essence as well.

You are at once a beating heart and a single heartbeat in this body called humanity.

Live forgiveness every day rather than just talk about it on Sunday.

Ask for nothing
and you will
receive much.

You are alone and all one, all at the same time.

Our world is always perfect. Salmon swimming upstream to their spawning site are mysteriously perfect. The swallows who show up on the same day century after century are perfect. Even the spider who knows how to build his web without going to web school is perfect. So, too, are you a part of that perfection.

The more you try to force something for your own benefit, the less you will enjoy what you are seeking so desperately.

Little, seemingly unconnected and meaningless events, viewed from the perspective of now, all led you to this very moment.

Everything is already here in the world. Where else would it be?

Your purpose is always about giving, loving and serving in some capacity.

You are a soul with a body rather than a body with a soul.

Allow yourself the luxury of believing in the divinity of your own soul.

Your very essence is an invisible intelligence. Your essence is in thought, where it is virtually impossible to have attachment.

Who you are is located in the dimensionless realm that we call your thoughts.

Creating money is just like
creating anything else in your life.
It involves not being attached to it,
and not giving it power over
your life in any way.

Suffering is always played out in form. It is not you who suffers, only the person you imagine yourself to be.

All you have become is the result of all you have thought.

Surrendering is an act of the heart.

❖

How do you surrender? Just let go.

You mustn't attempt to will anything. You need only be willing. Even though the sky will be different in a few hours, its present perfection and completeness is not deficient. You, too, are presently perfect and not deficient because you will be different tomorrow.

You are intelligence within your form, just as the rose is an intelligence that delivers the fragrance and appearance of a flower.

Abundance flows when we love what we are doing.

Everything you are currently against blocks you from abundance.

Willingness to use trust and knowing will come to you only through your thoughts.

Miracles can only happen when you get rid of the concept of "impossible" and allow yourself to experience the magic of knowing.

The first step toward
discarding a scarcity
mentality involves giving
thanks for everything that
you are and everything
that you have.

In your soul lies the entryway to the world of real magic.

To enter the realm of real magic you will have to suspend all thoughts of limitation and become a spiritual being first, a being who has no limitation in your inner domain where boundaries are nonexistent.

Acting as if you were already what you want to become and knowing that you can become it is the way to remove self-doubt and enter your real-magic kingdom.

There must be bliss and harmony within in order for you to know miracles.

Have in your mind that which would constitute a miracle for you. Get the vision. Suspend disbelief and skepticism. Allow yourself to take the journey toward real magic.

Examine what you believe to be impossible, and then change your beliefs.

We talk privately to God and
call it prayer. So, then why does
a return call seem so farfetched,
particularly if we believe that
there is some universal intelligence
out there that you are addressing?

Enlightenment is the quiet acceptance of what is.

When we love ourselves, we refuse to allow others to manage our emotions from afar. Forgiveness is our means to that end.

Forgiveness is the ability to give love away in the most difficult of circumstances.

Giving is the key to forgiving.

Some of the most despicable human behavior has been conducted in the name of "I'm only following the law," or "I'm only doing my job."

If we are to have magical bodies, we must have magical minds.

Treasure your physical being as a vehicle that houses your soul. Once you have the inner way, the outer way will follow.

We receive only that which we are willing to let in.

Create an inner harmony where your loving soul guides your physical behavior, rather than having your soul always come in second place.

Surrendering is trusting in the forces and principles that are always at work in this perfect universe.

The reality of life
speaks to us
in silence.

Forgiveness is man's highest achievement because it shows true enlightenment in action. It shows that one is in touch with the energy of love.

Judgement means that you view the world as *you* are, rather than as *it* is.

Love is giving and it has nothing to do with what you receive.

Your miracles are an inside job. Go there to create the magic that you seek in your life.

If you are committed to seeing your physical self with wonder and awe, and if you can know deep within that your invisible self wants the body it inhabits to be as healthy as possible, then you are a student who is ready.

Your limits are defined by the agreement you have made about what is possible. Change that agreement and you can dissolve all limits.

This total being called "human being" cannot function harmoniously when the components are in conflict.

The way to oneness seems to be through the path of inner harmony. The way to inner harmony is through silence.

The dying process in the physical world allows you to live.

There are no accidents in a perfect universe.

We are all part of an endless universe.

A few minutes spent in
total awe will contribute to
your spiritual awakening
faster than any
metaphysics course.

We all come from *no where* to *now here* to *no where*. It is all the same. It is all one.

Purpose is about giving yourself unconditionally and accepting what comes back with love, even if what comes back is not what you had anticipated.

Being a spiritual being involves being able to touch your invisible self.

In the dimensionless world of thought, everything is possible.

Go within to the peaceful solitude of your mind. It is there that you will discover God.

It is all perfect, this universe we are in. Slow down and enjoy it all.